HEALING CHICAGO

This book belongs to

_____

"Releasing the Ghost of Niggas Past"

Minister, Shaman & healer
Dominique Irene Graves

The Holistic Chef LLC

Copyright

2021 By

Dominique Irene Graves

The Holistic Chef LLC

Healing Worldwide In chicago Association

All rights reserved. No part of this publication may be reproduced or transmitted in any form, electronic or mechanical, including photocopy or recording without the written permission of the author.

ISBN:

For information and ordering, contact the

author: The Holistic Chef LLC

Info@holistic-chef.com

www.holistic-chef.com

Office Phone: (773) 982-6020

Chefnique_chicago & spiritual_holistic_chef

Keyword: Mizznique

Credits

I'd first and foremost like to thank my felt but unseen family who guided me since my arrival here through this entire journey to my divine higher self! My devoted ancestors especially my tete and my daddy who I love so much, my spirit guides and extraterrestrial family. I honor you for the sacrifices you made, the unconditional love you continue to pour into my very existence and the shield of protection you stand by so strongly. I'd also like to thank my soul teachers/family who magically appeared in my life at the right time... Dr Isa, Magickal lady duchess, Sapphire dragonfly & angel anita. Words can't explain my love and appreciation for you guys in assisting me with learning self love, trusting my intuition, strengthening me through my challenges and tests and simply being 100% who you are authentically which gave me and so many millions of other people faith and courage to be who they truly are as well. Next I'd like to thank my genuine family, friends and supporters who also have been with me through my journey of self discovery.

More importantly I'd like to thank my son Je'Marey for simply being you. Although you are one of my very first manifestations I wouldn't be living right now if it weren't for you! Every time I felt like I couldn't bare anymore of this world you looked me in my eyes and smiled and gave me every reason to stay and fight. Despite every struggle and challenge we went through, you amazingly stayed the happiest kid I've ever seen. Even when I tried my best to shield my depression from you, you always knew intuitively when I needed your hugs, a kiss or for you to say I'm the best mommy in the world or I'm the best chef in the world lol. Sometimes I look at you with tears in
my eyes and thank the universe every chance I get for sending me such a strong developed soul to walk this journey with. I can't wait to see what amazing things you're gonna do this lifetime!

To my granny bates. My angel on earth. I thank you for loving me in the way that I needed at the perfect time. My first definition of unconditional FEMININE energy and love. I never knew how uncomfortable I was with receiving genuine affection until I met you. I remember I had an extreme breakdown and you grabbed me and held me so tight, I tried to break free but you wouldn't let me go and told me to give you all my pain and I just cried and cried until I couldn't anymore. Words can't describe how much that moment allowed me to not only be conscious of the chains I held within myself and my heart but to also start the process of breaking free of those chains. You made me feel safe in a way that I never felt, loved in a way I never thought was even possible and valued even more than I valued myself at that time. I thank you, love you and appreciate you being in my life.

Last but not least I'd like to thank myself. Dominique Irene Graves. Ever since your very existence you've been going through trials and tribulations and here you are now. Walking in your truth! Being a brave enough soul to work consistently at shedding all the conditions that was learned, painfully going through the process of healing yourself, being true to who you are regardless of what others say or felt and passing every test the universe sent to you in order for you to grow and get to this very point. Your divine FEMININE badass self!

"So the last shall be first, and the first last: for many be called, but few chosen."

Matthew 20:16

My love letter to my higher self, ancestors and Divine feminine....

Dear higher self, my beloved ancestors both known and unknown, my spirit guides and my esoteric family......

    If you would've told me 10 years ago how peaceful, powerful, blessed and abundant my life would be right now I wouldn't have believed you. In fact I was always reminded of how special I am, how magickal I am, how beautiful I am or how pure my heart is many times throughout my life from childhood to adulthood from strangers, earth angels etc. I just couldn't see what others saw in me.

They saw beautiful lights radiating from my aura , a massive and highly unique caring heart, passion for helping others, a big bright future ahead of me, unconditional love for life and people.... But all I saw when I looked at myself (If and when I had the courage to stare at my reflection) was shame, unattractiveness, a unhealed inner child, alllll my insecurities and any and all the pain, emptiness and hurt I ever endured since arriving on this planet 9/18/1990. My journey up until this point have been filled with lessons, many of which I had to repeat several times because I'm hardheaded asffff, including toxic relationships both personal and professional, homelessness, putting everyone else over my self, being a pushover, lack of self love, abuse, procrastination etc. Healing is one of the most difficult things required for each and every one of us. Yes you deal with resurfaced issues such as childhood traumas, sexual traumas, poverty, things we intentionally and unintentionally sweep under the rug, voids from absentee parents.... I can only imagine the struggles and disappointments we ALL individually and collectively experienced together in this life time and the lifetimes before. I am here to be a witness, A vessel for you, a sign of the universe that no matter what you went through, no matter what toxicity you were born into, no matter what pains you felt in your heart... None of that is a reflection of who YOU are as a person and what you mean to me and this world! That man or woman who hurt you rather it be your mother, your father, your aunt, your husband, your ex boyfriend, the person who took your innocence as a child, your uncle who knew he had no business touching you in the first place! That has everything to do with them and what they are and absolutely nothing to do with who you have the potential to be! I had to get to a point where I could barely fucking walk or even function normally with all the baggage I been walking around carrying all these years! All these lifetimes! Nevertheless every singlestep of the way I had assistance from my spiritual army. All the times I thought I was alone I was surrounded by love and protection in the midst of the storms.... I dedicate this letter to you to thank you for your unconditional love, guidance, gifts and strength in walking and sometimes (most times) carrying me on my journey to self love, discovery and acceptance of myself and who I am entirely.

To my beloved divine feminine,

To every woman who has ever went through ANY form of abuse,

"When you are evolving to your higher self, the road seems lonely but you're simply shedding the energies that no longer match the frequency of your destiny ".

Table of Contents

- **Chapter 1 Why is womb healing important? (Page 12) Chapter 2: Generational curses (Page 15)**
- **Chapter 3: Sexual harrassment (Page 20)**
- **Chapter 4: Toxic exes (Page 24)**
- **Chapter 5: Prostitution (Page 30)**
- **Chapter 6: Miscarriage, abortion and conceiving**
- **issues (Page 36)**
- **Chapter 7: Childhood trauma (Page 40)**
- **Chapter 8: Health and STD (Page 44)**
- **Chapter 9: Detox baths (Page 49)**
- **Chapter 10: Womb alters (Page 57)**
- **Chapter 11: Moon rituals for womb and yoni clearing (Page 60)**
- **Chapter 12: Herbs and crystals (Page 66)**
- **Chapter 13: Bonus Chapter: (Excerpt from next book) Mirror magic & powerful affirmations for healing the divine feminine (Page 70)**
- **Chapter 14: My personal playlist (women empowerment music) (Page 73)**

Foreword

Let's first talk about this book title. Other than the fact that this title was given to me from spirit, the root word and where it stemmed from is the basis of my book. Meaning healing has more to do with our past and the conditions WE as our ancestors had to endure and are still dealing with in today's society. Rather you believe it or not a lot of you guys have reincarnated 100's of thousands of times and just because a person dies doesn't mean the pain, suffering, neglect or abuse died with that physical body at the time. Your souls have gone through so much and when things aren't corrected, healed or even when our frequency isn't heightened we reincarnate and have to deal with these unhealed conditions yet again. Over and over and over again. It can be as simple as banishing a poverty generational curse so that your blood line won't keep being born into low income housing and choosing to stay there cause they too scared to be in a uncomfortable situation or they don't think they deserve more cause all they grew up seeing was lack or as complex as confronting your abuser (we'll discuss this further in CHAPTER 3), confronting any energies that your soul could have violated in past lifetimes, releasing any bockages you gave yourself out of fear of what happened in the past so that your children and grandchildren don't have to worry about being violated when they come back to earth. I want y'all to read this book with an open mind! This journey won't be easy but it's absolutely necessary for the advancement of mother earth and the advancements of your souls! She will raise her frequency regardless so i suggest you take this shit seriously.

P.S. Leave your sensitivity at the door. I'm not judging any of you all but sugarcoating aint it, not for a task as hard as this one. We must face these things bravely and honestly and hold ourselves and everyone accountable for today's conditions so that we can do better and be better. Love each of you dearly and unconditionally! Now let's goooooooo

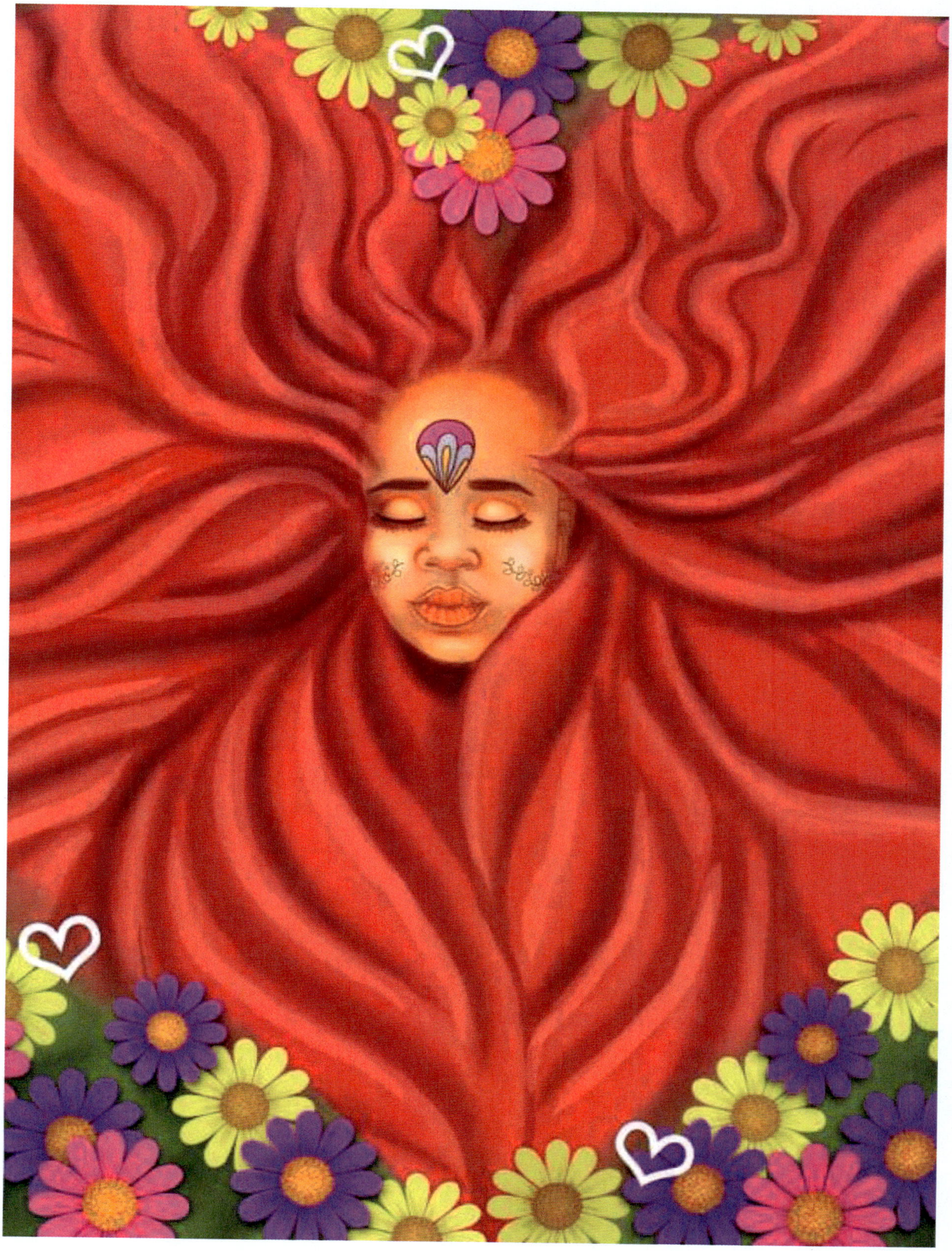

01
CHAPTER

What is womb healing & why is it important?

01

Chapter 1:

What is the womb healing exactly? Of course we know it's a place that births new life into the world but it's also a spiritual space of the all knowing, the direct connection from god. It's an important part of any womans transformation as your womb is your center of creation. It's amazing how much you can manifest and attract to you from a heal perspective. Life changing. It will enable you to attract your true goddess energy and do the works of god! It carries its own chakra and is a mirror of your soul's life events from the current and past. Ancient womb healing has the ability help you transform relationships, resolves generational issues, promotes your creativity, reducing anxiety, handle stress effectively, helps clear your body of negivity energies and spirits and so much more. While on this journey it's important to have guidance or a professional to help guide you and be a support through this process. Also utilize your ancestors, that's part of the reason they're around ready to be of assistance and help ypu with this task but you have to openly give them permission because they don't have freewill. Call on them! You'll be surprised how much stronger you are after your spiritual army is fully activated. You can use techniques such as meditation, yoga, sigils, self love magic spells (if you're into that) etc.

What can cause womb trauma?

Sexual trauma that can be passed down through generational wombs, abuse at a young age, very complicated births, STD's, prostitution and many other factors we'll discuss in this book. The important thing is that you're taking the iniative to start the proces to heal your internal and external world.

Some things you can do to help heal is talk to your womb, getting a womb massage, take relaxing baths regularly, focus on yourself and not external forces like your family, boyfriend etc. This is your time to love yourself and forgive yourself and others for any and all trauma that was caused known and unknown.

DAILY JOURNAL

DATE:

02
CHAPTER

Generational curses

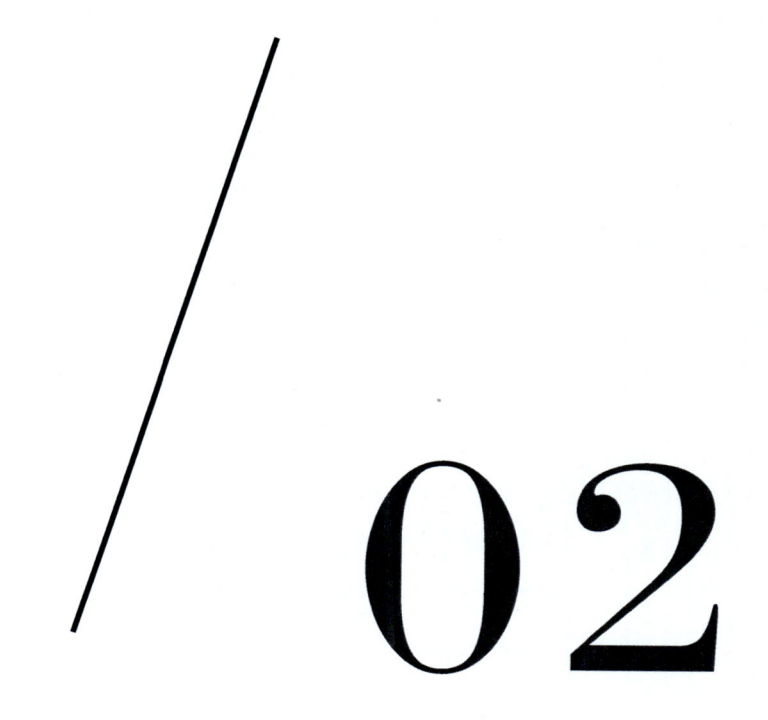

/ 02

Chapter 2:

Generational curses describe the effect on a person of things that their ancestors did, believed, or practiced in the past and a consequence of an ancestor's actions, beliefs and wromgdoimgs be passed down. Some examples are addictions, mental illnesses, physical illnesses, poverty and many more.

How to break destructive patterns

Create healthy relationships with others, have healthy boundaries, even traveling can assist with this seeing as though being exposed to the world and experiences and other ways of life and living can certainly make you more aware of things and the way you think. You can free your whole bloodline, kids even siblings from experiencing certain issues or traumas because you've closed that chapter no matter how many lifetimes it's been in existance. Generational curses can also be spells or roots a person can curse your blooodline with in which case you need to contact a professional to help you deal with this matter.

Whatever you can visually see that's been holding your family back do the opposite. Yes things may be harder especially when forces are working against you but it's worth it and absolutely necessary. If you're the first college graduate, first business owner or even the first to build generation wealth then it was meant to be that way. Free your ancestors!

What are some generational curses you see in your family and how can you change this?

DAILY JOURNAL

DATE:

DAILY JOURNAL

DATE:

03
CHAPTER

Sexual harrassment

03

Chapter 3:

Being violated in any way can cause so much trauma to the womb. Sexual harassment or rape can make a woman shut down completely in regards to trusting a man or any person or be excessive with having sex with multiple partners to mask the emotions they feel inside. Everyone deals with trauma differently and I encourage you to try to face your abusers by writing a letter or even stating what you feel outloud, whatever method you choose just get it out. Feel it. Express it. You may not be ready to forgive the one who committed violence against you or someone you know, but once you have it you'll feel like you're on top of the world. Its not for them but for you to face your emotions so that it will no longer rule your former self. Only way to get on the other side of the bridge is to walk over it. Good luck ladies...

DAILY JOURNAL

DATE:

DAILY JOURNAL

DATE:

CHAPTER 04

Toxic Exes

04

Chapter 4:

Ouuuu chile! Most if not all of us women had moments where we dated and courted men we had no business being with from when we were young ladies still learning the value of women to when we became adults. My uncle used to say "Sizzly dizzle" or "Hot fish in the frying pan" to me and my friends all the time when i was a teenager lol. That's his way of noticing when I started smelling myself as he says i guess but Anywho, remember i said we hold everything in our wombs so when we have sex a part of that man leaves energy with us. Depending on that man's karma is how
much or less you and your life can be affected by this act of sexual pleasure that took place. That baby daddy we are embarrassed to claim, that one night stand that ended up being an 18 year
night stand and any and every man you ever let enter your divine internal world. Whatever it is, it's important to detox these energies. Ever notice how low your life becomes when being in a relationship that wasn't so good for you. This can equally happen to men if we women don't clear our aura. Money could decrease, start losing weight, drama coming from everywhere, developing unhealthy habits etc. Especially if you're at a new height in your life where you did some healing and are trying to attract king-like energy and find you're still attracting the scrubs TLC was referring to in their song. It's because of the past that has to be cleared. I've been through it all in regards to energy and I can tell you that it can be a life or death situation with these energies. To be honest sex is used so loosely these days, we technically only supposed to be having sex to conceive and/or do some powerful manifesting but thats another conversation on another day. For now I
want you guys to do the work to release the energies and purify your womb for you and your generations that you may or maynot carry in that very same womb so that they can have a chance to start fresh without dealing with your lingering acts.

P.S. For future reference pay attention to how your body energy and health feels after sex with anyone. It'll tell you everything you need to know queen.

Black walnut bath

FYI: All tips, tea baths etc can be purchased from my website www.holistic-chef.com or by contacting me personally at info@holistic-chef.com. You can also administer these things yourself but SAFELY! Please do your research ladies.

This bath was designed to remove and break toxic relationships, heartbreaks, toxic bonds, soul ties and sexual partners and any of their emotional baggage that was left behind out of your womb. Here's how you make it. I usually use 9 walnuts, I boil them for about 4 hours adding water as it cooks down which will turn this into a dark black liquid. Clean your space, bathe or shower first and clean your body thoroughly! You will then make your bath, pour the contents in and relax. With your own determination and manifestations, the ability to be clear and ready with the mindset and power of your verbalizations and the will to actually let go will change your life. This is a very powerful
bath and I advise you to do this only when you're ready.

FEELINGS EVALUATION BEFORE BATH

How do you feel your past toxic connections have an affect on your life today? How has it helped or hindered your development as a woman?

Before your bath: How do you feel? What and who do you want to release and why? (Use additional paper if needed)

FEELINGS EVALUATION AFTER BATH

How do you feel after taking your bath? 1-2 days

How do you feel now? 7 days

DAILY JOURNAL

DATE:

DAILY JOURNAL

DATE:

CHAPTER 05 / Prostitution / 05

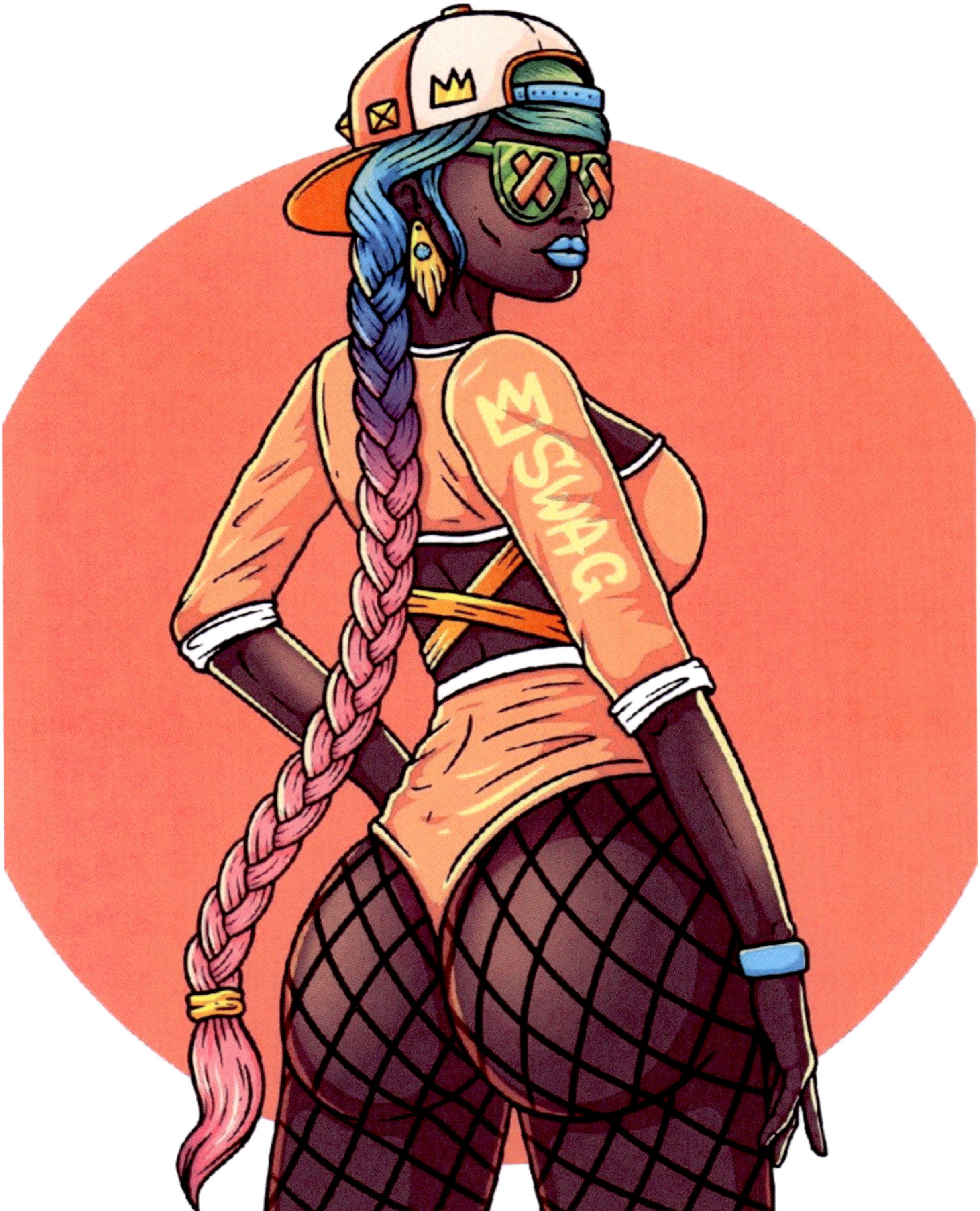
SWAG

Chapter 5:
Prostitution

Because of the various life forces and different experiences that sex prostitution carries, this is one of the worst kinds of trauma the womb can suffer from. As stated in the previous chapter every time you merge with someone you take on that energy and bodily fluids. And frankly most men who indulge in that lifestyle does it often with various prostitutes so the damage is much more intense sometimes than having sex with an average man. They use sex as an outlet for whatever can be going wrong in their life and give it all to you. Your body has living cells which means it can hear, feel and even remember everything that has and will happen on a physical, spiritual and emotional level. I'm certainly not judging what or how you got to this stage in your life but merely to show you the damage you're currently doing or have done in the past. Like all traumas this isn't one we can just move from in our lives when we decide to change, we must face what got us there in the first place. I recommend the walnut bath and self love healing work.

How did prositution effect your life and your families life? How did it make you feel? How do you feel now?

DAILY JOURNAL

DATE:

DAILY JOURNAL

DATE:

06
CHAPTER

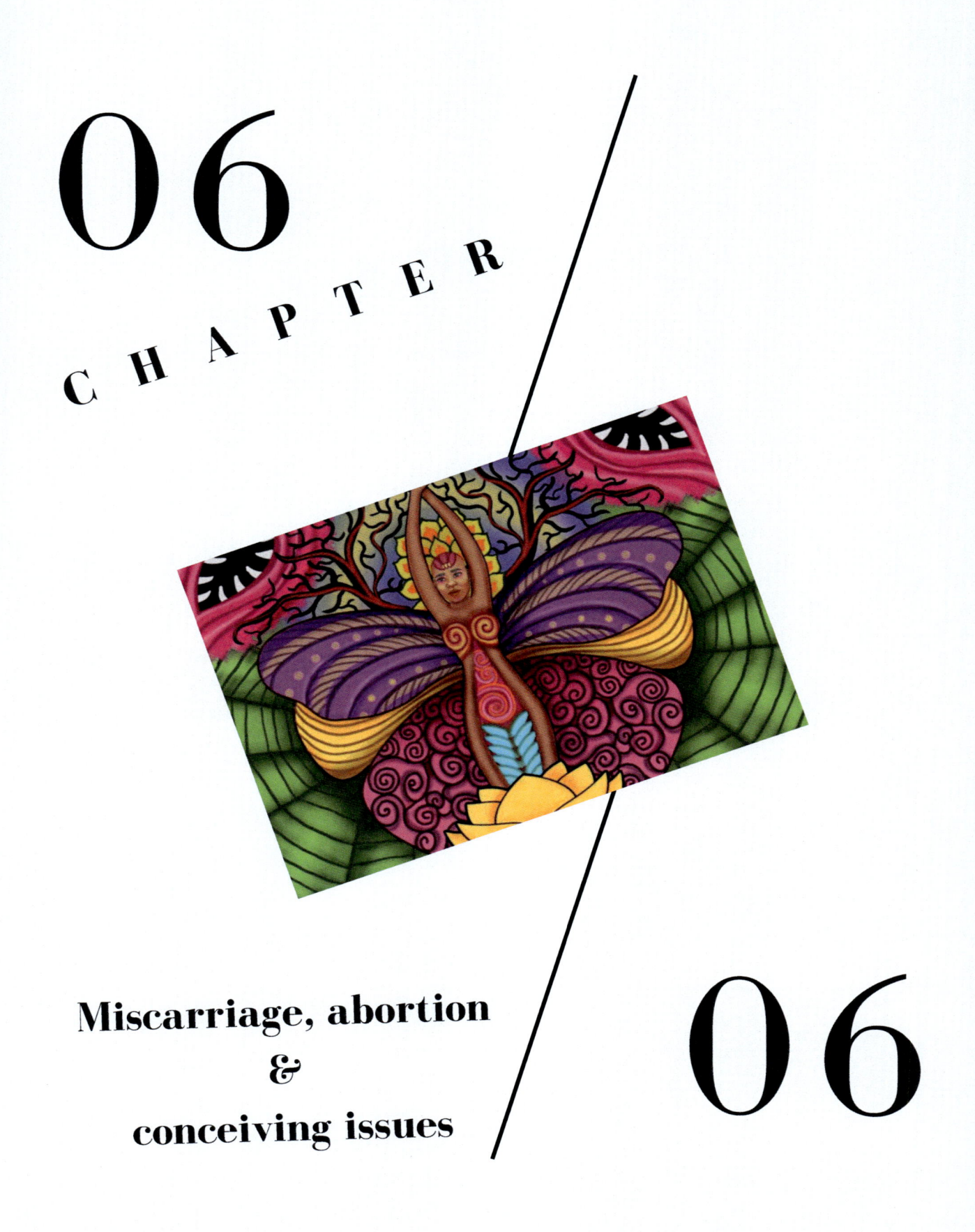

Miscarriage, abortion & conceiving issues

06

Chapter 6:

Abortions and miscarriages can cause womb trauma and can cause the body to not be able to conceive. Your womb remembers and feels everything, the anaesthesia or even the medicines used can cause trauma as well. Just as you'll never forget an act of violence that took place, your womb is the same. Even giving birth can be traumatic from unhealthy food and emotions you can experience during pregnancy. If you're going through emotions from having an abortion at anytime or from a miscarriage it can have you feeling sad, afraid, angry and/or inadequate which can be a blockage. Start by forgiving yourself and talking to your womb and your unborn child's soul to help ease the tension that can be stored in your womb. Tell your womb and child that you love and cherish them and am working to provide a clean and loving space. Those who have conception issues can also do this excercise. A few herbs that will help raise the probability of conception is red raspberry leaf, wild jamroot and red diatomaceous earth.

DAILY JOURNAL

DATE:

DAILY JOURNAL

DATE:

CHAPTER 07

Childhood Trauma

KEYPOINTS

- Neglect/abandonment
- Sexual trauma
- Physical abuse/emotional abuse Bullying
- Divorce
- Substance abuse
- Mental illness
- Violence against your mother

Chapter 7:

All of these key points can affect a child in so may ways. There's so many kids experiencing traumans and processing adult emotions way beforee they should have to. Recognize the issues and trauma you have went through that you can be projecting onto your child. For example divorce, It's bad enough that they have to deal with the family separating but dragging them into your bullshit because you're mad at the dad is not good at all. You don't want your child resenting you in any kind of way. Parents are our first role models and it will set the stage for how they feel about life in the future and conduct relationships with others.

Bullying and violence against their mom is another key point that children deal with that can affect adulthood. They can grow up bullying other, not having control of their emotions where they get in bad situations often or fighting women because that's what dad did.

I know it can be hard when you're in the process of trying to heal but atleast be mindful of the fact that hurt people hurt people, even you. Find out where the anger stems from so that you can be a more nurturing mom. And please watch what you say to your chidren, that may be how you were raised but if you see that growing up the insults your family gave you fucked you up, why keep the cycle going. Apologize to that baby and let them know you're working on being better. And stop beating that damn baby too! I don't know who I'm talking to but you heard what i said. Nip it in the bud asap! Love you...

DAILY JOURNAL

DATE:

DAILY JOURNAL

DATE:

CHAPTER 08

Health, STD & clothing

Chapter 8:

Having hygiene issues can lead to infections in the yoni that can also lead to issues in the womb as well as wearing clothes too tight. Ungarments need to be loose or not worn at lol. Let that pumpum breathe girl. Sexual transmitted disease of any kind can also hurt the womb and can actually cause conceiving issues if left untreated.

DIY Yoni wash

witch hazel
rose water
almond oil
castile soap
essential oils (lavender and chamomile)

DIY Yoni wash

aloe vera
vinegar
castile soap
extra virgin olive oil
essential oils

DAILY JOURNAL

DATE:

DAILY JOURNAL

DATE:

DAILY JOURNAL

DATE:

CHAPTER 09

Detox Baths

09

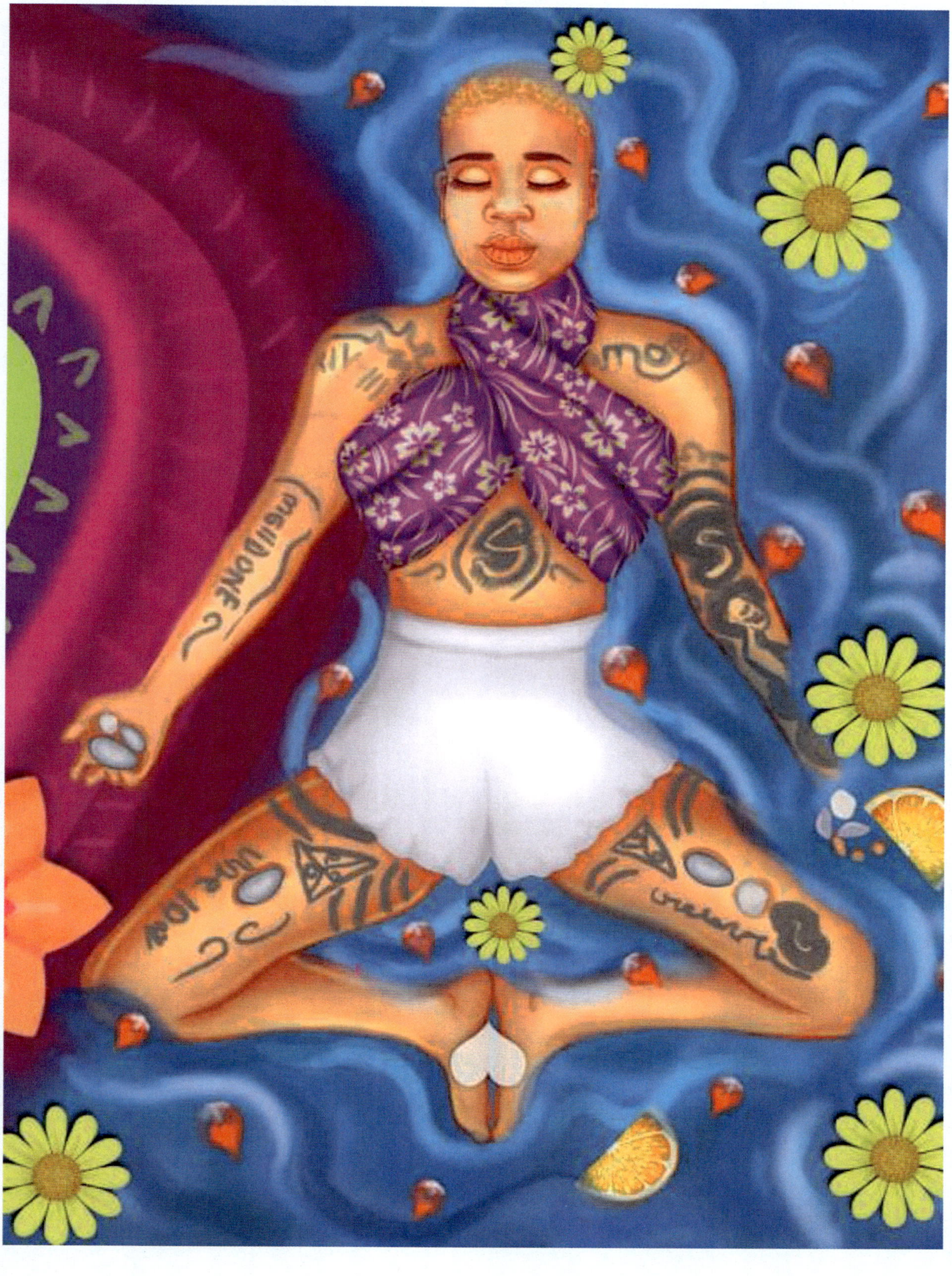

ANTI-INFLAMMATORY BATH

TOTAL TIME: 30 MINUTES

INGREDIENTS

1/4 CUP MUSTARD BATH
1 CUP BAKING SODA

RESULTS:

ANTI-INFLAMMATORY BATH

TOTAL TIME:
30 MINUTES

INGREDIENTS

1/4 CUP MUSTARD BATH
1 CUP BAKING SODA

DETOXIFICATION

**TOTAL TIME:
30 MINUTES**

1 BOTTLE HYDROGEN PEROXIDE
1 TBSP FRESHLY GRATED GINGER

DRAW OUT IMPURITIES

**TOTAL TIME:
30 MINUTES**

1 CUP SEA SALT
1 CUP EPSOM SALT
2 CUPS BAKING SODA
10 DROPS EUCALYPTUS
ESSENTIAL OIL

DAILY JOURNAL

DATE:

DAILY JOURNAL

DATE:

CHAPTER 10

Womb Alters

What is an altar?

Altars are used everywhere but is most recognized in religious practices to channel spiritual energies, love and peace into your home. A list of things you can use are crystals for healing the womb, a pink or white candle, water, fresh beautiful flowers, yoni herbs etc. Lay it on a table with a cloth or on a designated spot on the floor and feed it daily, talk to your higher god feminine energy, love it, feel the energy purifying from the inside out, I usually write love letters to my higher self also.

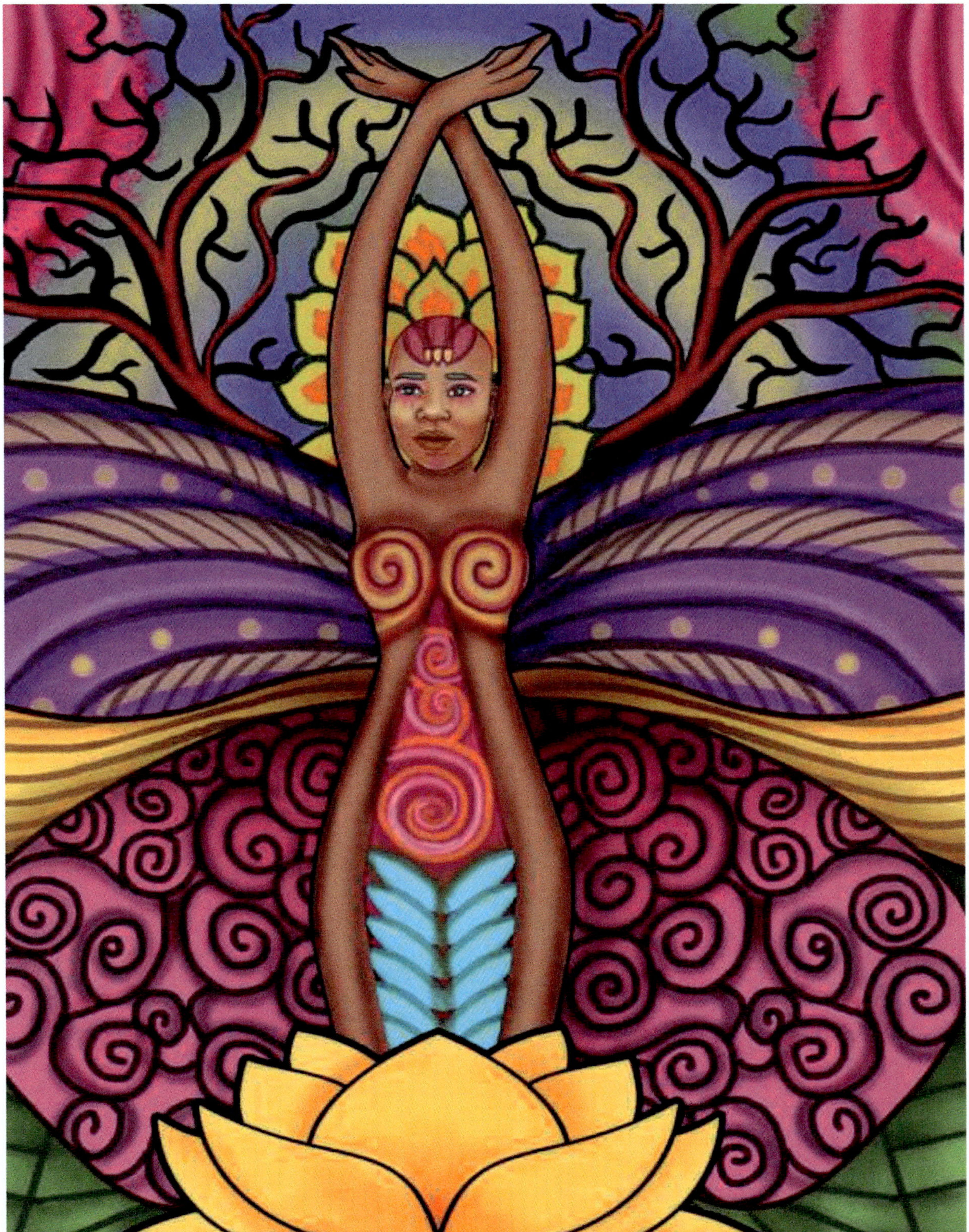

CHAPTER 11

Moon rituals for womb & yoni clearing

Use the lunar phases and moon phase meanings to see what its best for. Think of the full moon as your full amazon carts lol. I'm joking. Think of a cup if its full of shit how can you put more shit in it, It'll just spill over. You have to pour it out and clean the residue to make room for the new. A new moon is a new cup ready for you to put your new manifestations in.

Lunar Phases 2021

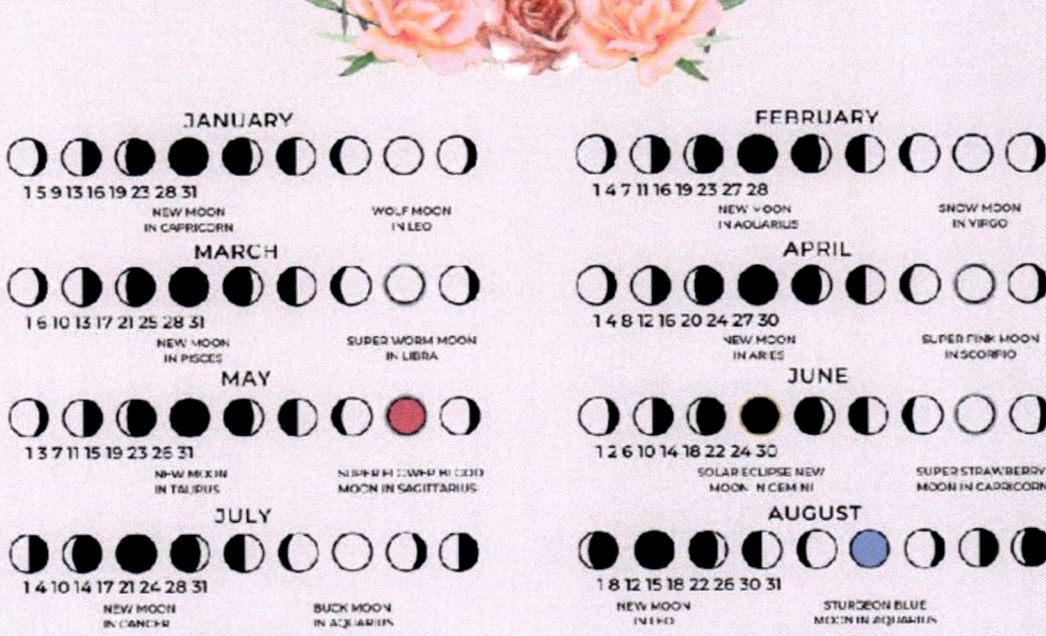

JANUARY
1 5 9 13 16 19 23 28 31
NEW MOON IN CAPRICORN
WOLF MOON IN LEO

FEBRUARY
1 4 7 11 16 19 23 27 28
NEW MOON IN AQUARIUS
SNOW MOON IN VIRGO

MARCH
1 6 10 13 17 21 25 28 31
NEW MOON IN PISCES
SUPER WORM MOON IN LIBRA

APRIL
1 4 8 12 16 20 24 27 30
NEW MOON IN ARIES
SUPER PINK MOON IN SCORPIO

MAY
1 3 7 11 15 19 23 26 31
NEW MOON IN TAURUS
SUPER FLOWER BLOOD MOON IN SAGITTARIUS

JUNE
1 2 6 10 14 18 22 24 30
SOLAR ECLIPSE NEW MOON IN GEMINI
SUPER STRAWBERRY MOON IN CAPRICORN

JULY
1 4 10 14 17 21 24 28 31
NEW MOON IN CANCER
BUCK MOON IN AQUARIUS

AUGUST
1 8 12 15 18 22 26 30 31
NEW MOON IN LEO
STURGEON BLUE MOON IN AQUARIUS

SEPTEMBER
1 7 10 13 16 20 24 28 31
NEW MOON IN VIRGO
CORN HARVEST MOON IN PISCES

OCTOBER
1 6 9 13 16 20 24 28 31
NEW MOON IN LIBRA
HUNTER'S MOON IN ARIES

NOVEMBER
1 4 7 11 15 19 24 28 30
NEW MOON IN SCORPIO
BEAVER BLOOD MOON IN TAURUS

DECEMBER
1 4 7 10 14 19 23 27 31
SOLAR ECLIPSE NEW MOON IN SAGITTARIUS
COLD MOON IN GEMINI

Lunar Phases
2022

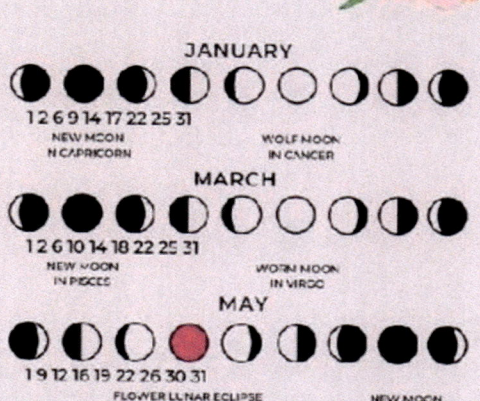

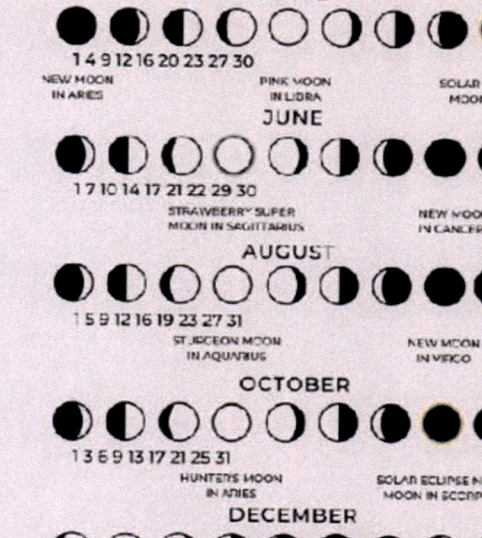

JANUARY
1 2 6 9 14 17 22 25 31
NEW MOON IN CAPRICORN
WOLF MOON IN CANCER

FEBRUARY
1 4 8 11 16 19 23 27 28
NEW MOON IN AQUARIUS
SNOW MOON IN LEO

MARCH
1 2 6 10 14 18 22 25 31
NEW MOON IN PISCES
WORM MOON IN VIRGO

APRIL
1 4 9 12 16 20 23 27 30
NEW MOON IN ARIES
PINK MOON IN LIBRA
SOLAR ECLIPSE NEW MOON IN TAURUS

MAY
1 9 12 16 19 22 26 30 31
FLOWER LUNAR ECLIPSE MOON IN SCORPIO
NEW MOON IN GEMINI

JUNE
1 7 10 14 17 21 22 29 30
STRAWBERRY SUPER MOON IN SAGITTARIUS
NEW MOON IN CANCER

JULY
1 7 10 13 17 20 24 28 31
BUCK SUPER MOON IN CAPRICORN
NEW MOON IN LEO

AUGUST
1 5 9 12 16 19 23 27 31
STURGEON MOON IN AQUARIUS
NEW MOON IN VIRGO

SEPTEMBER
1 3 7 10 14 17 21 25 30
CORN/HARVEST MOON IN PISCES
NEW MOON IN LIBRA

OCTOBER
1 3 6 9 13 17 21 25 31
HUNTER'S MOON IN ARIES
SOLAR ECLIPSE NEW MOON IN SCORPIO

NOVEMBER
1 4 8 12 16 20 23 27 30
BEAVER LUNAR ECLIPSE MOON IN TAURUS
NEW MOON IN SAGITTARIUS

DECEMBER
1 8 12 16 20 23 27 30 31
COLD MOON IN GEMINI
NEW MOON IN CAPRICORN

SMALLRPPLES.COM

Moon Phase Activities
MOON ENERGY GUIDE

PERSONAL ENERGY: OUTWARD FOCUSED

PERSONAL ENERGY: INWARD FOCUSED

NEW MOON
Self care, Journaling & Intention Setting

FULL MOON
Ceremony, Rituals, Divination & Manifestation

WAXING CRESCENT
Yoga, Gentle Exercise & Connecting With Nature

WANING GIBBOUS
Creative Pursuits, Hobbies & Reading

FIRST QUARTER
Social Events, Connection With Others, Action in Career & Business

THIRD QUARTER
Releasing, Cord Cutting & Energy Clearing

WAXING GIBBOUS   **WANING CRESCENT**
Meditation, Quiet Contemplation, Mindfulness & Reflection, Planning
Sacred Communion for the Journey
With the Divine Ahead

SMALLRIPPLES.COM

Moon Phase Meanings

NEW MOON
The New Moon is associated with new beginnings, renewed strength and is the perfect time for intention setting.

FULL MOON
The moon shines brightly in the sky and is bursting with energy. This is the perfect time for manifestation practices and rituals.

WAXING CRESCENT
As the moon begins to illuminate again, this is a great time to set goals and work on your inner strength.

WANING GIBBOUS
Though she is starting to wane, the moon is still very powerful at this time and we can still use her energy for manifestation.

FIRST QUARTER
The moon is in a state of balance, now is the time to start taking action and bring those goals & intentions to fruition.

LAST QUARTER
We find ourselves at a place of balance again during the Last Quarter. This is a time for letting go of what no longer serves us.

WAXING GIBBOUS
At this point in the lunar cycle, we can really feel the strength of the moon. This is the time to take a little pause and reserve our energy for the climax of the full moon.

WANING CRESCENT
The waning moon signals that it is time to retreat back into our inner world. Take the time to journal, meditate and hone in on your intuition. Where should you go next?

SMALLRIPPLES.COM

The Cycle of The Moon

NEW MOON

WANING CRESCENT / WAXING CRESCENT

LAST QUARTER

FIRST QUARTER

WANING GIBBOUS / WAXING GIBBOUS

FULL MOON

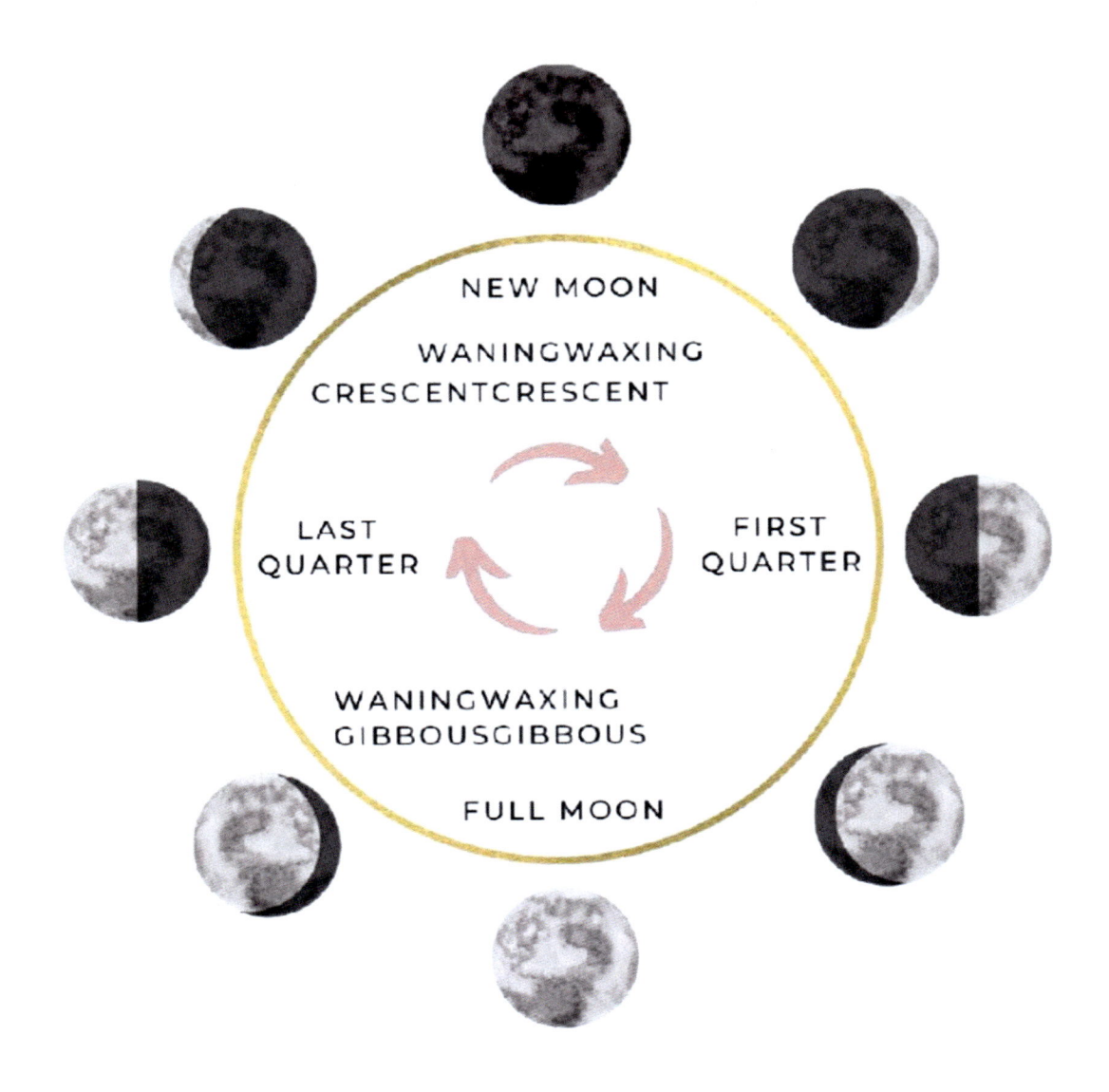

SMALLRIPPLES.COM

CHAPTER 12

Herbs & crystals

/12

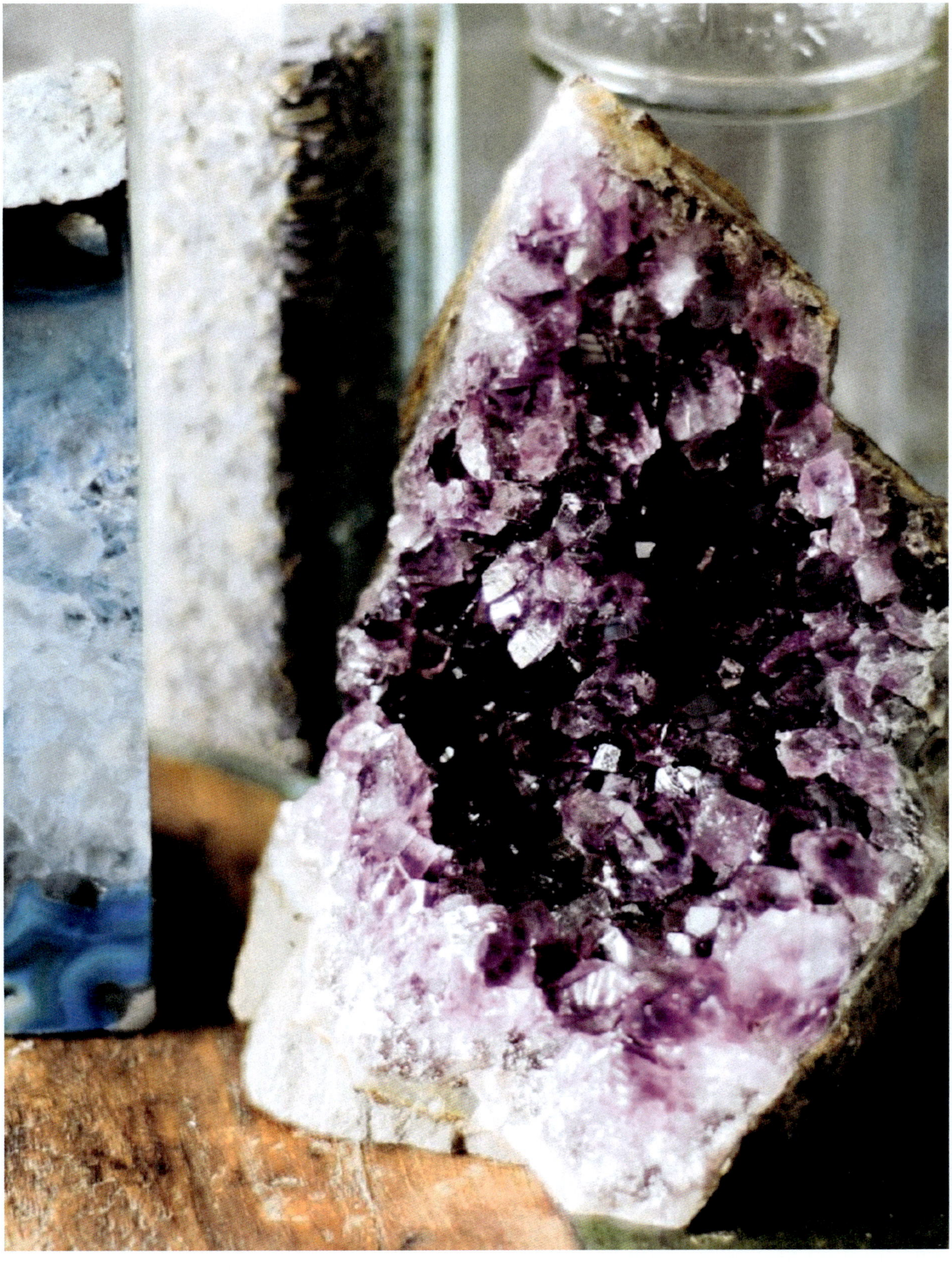

Herbs for the womb

Cleansing — Basil, Rose, Milk thistle, Motherwort, Calendula

Uterus strengthening — Rosemary, Ginseng, Astragalus, Yarrow, Ashwaganda,

Digestion Support — Lavender, Lemon balm, Cirtus peels, Mint, Lemon grass

Detox — Marigold, Motherwart, Ginger

Crystals for the womb

Rose quartz — Associated with a mother's love, balances and heals emotions, promotes self love and confidence.

Moon stone — egulates menstrual cycles, boost fertility, aids in conception and enhances sexual connection.

Green aventurine — Stengthens your connection to mother earth, helps prevent miscarriages and assists with stabilizing your emotions.

Red Garnet — Balances sex drive, assist with deepening romantic love and helps brig creative powers to fruition.

Carnelian — Stimulates, balances and heals women's reproductive systems, eases PMS & irregular cycles and boost fertility.

Rhodonite — Boost self-worth, enables unconditional love and respect for the lady.

13

BONUS CHAPTER

Mirror magic & powerful affirmations for healing the divine feminine

EXCERPT FROM MY NEXT BOOK

/ 13

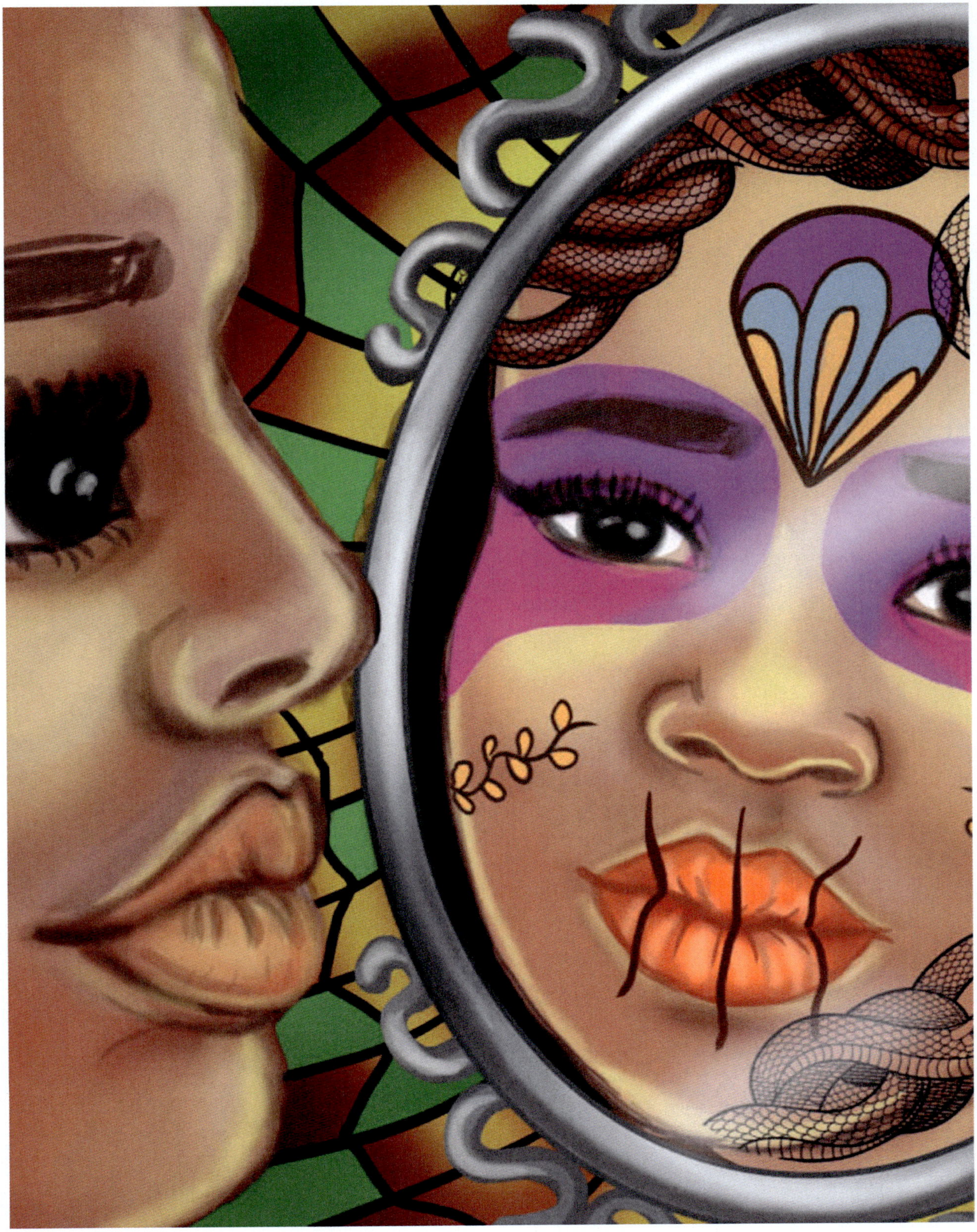

"What do you see when you look in the mirror?

Mirror magic is a way to work on your confidence, give yourself self love and even can be used to see yourself in a past life. Mirrors reflect back to us the energy we give it. Connect to this energy to create magic!

It use to be a time in my life that I barely looked in the mirror because I didn't like what i saw. People would approach me daily telling me how beautiful I am or how happy I always was or that I should be a model but at the time I didn't see what they saw nor did I actually feel the emotions I showed to the world regularly until mirror magic saved my life. Self love is such an important factor when healing the divine feminine. When you feel genuinely good inside, love yourself and know your true worth it makes everything in life so much easier and exciting. I don't care how you grew up, what your mom told you, what that man told you or what those mean kids said when you were young. I'm here to tell you you are beautiful, you are loved and you are valued. It's time to put that crown on your head where it belongs honey. Walk in your power and feel the divine energy covering your body! I want you to go to a mirror and repeat these statements daily.

Gaze at your relection and enter a trance state. (Normalize not looking in the mirror obsessing over small imperfections that no one else sees but you.) Give yourself an unconditional loving gaze. The unconditional love that god gives to us. No flaws just perfection right?

Say "Good morning beautiful" to yourself looking deeply in your eyes and call out 5 things you love and/or are grateful about yourself and really mean it!

14

Women empowerment

MY MUSIC PLAYLIST

14

Frankie Beverly & mayes (Lady of magic
Beyonce (Run the world) (Feeling myself)
Diana Gordon (Woman)
Destiny's child (Independent women)
India Arie (Video)
Beyonce (Flawless)
Alicia keys (Superwoman)
Mary J. Blige (Good woman down)
Estelle (Conqueror)
Foxy Brown (Big bad mama)
Janet Jackson (Nasty)
Janelle Monae & Erykah badu (QUEEN)
Cardi B & Meghan the stallion (WAP)
SZA & Kendrick lamar (Doves in the wind)
Lil Kim (Queen bitch)
Leikeli47 (Attitude)

Made in the USA
Columbia, SC
12 August 2022